This collection gets into your bones and stays. Rooted in marsh and mud, these poems keen with a somber beauty. Here is an unflinching family portrait, a tender collage of boyhood, and ultimately an ode to what home makes of us, all tuned to the particular frequency of McDonough's potent lyric. This is a gifted young poet and a beautiful debut.

—SAFIYA SINCLAIR, author of *How to Say Babylon*, winner of the National Book Critics Circle Award

Max McDonough's *Python with a Dog Inside It* deserves wide attention and the highest of praise. Its uncanny juxtapositions identify submerged moments of family and individual distress, as well as equally arresting disclosures of love. Its images regularly arrive in jump-cuts that reveal and transform, more than any sequential narrative could, emotional territories not available to usual ways of navigating. McDonough's investigations take the reader inside a sense of location that's precarious and charged: "...shadows of moth-flutter shrinking as night pries open its beak. The harsh links// between transmission towers. The sleeved white fire of black cables running a distance/ farther than any child could try." Such precise articulations of anxious need— through sensory image, sound, rhythm and syntax— are utterly absorbing, as the scenes move in and out of self, forward and backward in time, with the poems' own logic of echoing patterns and a voice that makes a whole out of the shattering, glittering pieces of a particular life. Such clarity of vision is how the best of poetry makes our own lives feel clearer too.

—DEBRA NYSTROM, author of *Night Sky Frequencies: New and Selected Poems*

The poems in *Python with a Dog Inside It* pulse with barbed beauty and fraught intimacy. By turns earthy and tender, brutal and unflinching, McDonough illuminates the hidden truths of both "suburban woods" and domestic home like a flashlight throwing darkness into relief. Tracing the legacy of family and the ghosts of what we witness, these poems ask, "does violence live in the genes, / their story telling itself / in the dormant voice / of a seed"? They will make you confront what latent history swirls in your own veins, daring to be repeated, rebuked, remade.

—ALINA GRABOWSKI, author of
Women and Children First

I've been waiting for a book from Max McDonough, and I'm so happy it's finally here. McDonough writes with astonishing precision, toggling lyric and narrative desires with exquisite poetic execution. *Python with a Dog Inside It* is a brutal and beautiful book that captures the fraught landscapes of familial trauma with striking diction and unforgettable imagery. The psychological impulse in this stunning collection ricochets and pings inside the violent transference from the personal to pastoral backdrops like the bloodworms breeding in "shoal water / slick with dimly shimmering husks, reproductive confetti / that wallowed up, smacked of semen on my tongue like hot syrup in the dark, familiar, alien." McDonough writes poems that needle, glimmer, and thrash. This stunning debut left me in awe, enthralled by a singular voice that bears witness to terror with tremendous tenderness, salvaging the ache with survival.

—TIANA CLARK, author of *I Can't Talk About the Trees Without the Blood*, winner of the Kate Tufts Discovery Award

PYTHON WITH A DOG INSIDE IT

PYTHON WITH
A DOG INSIDE IT

POEMS

MAX McDONOUGH

BLACK LAWRENCE PRESS

Black Lawrence Press

Executive Editor: Diane Goettel

Interior Design: Zoe Norvell

Cover Artwork: "The Collision Series 701" by Luca Brandi

Excerpt from Collected Poems, James Wright, c 1971 by James Wright. Published by Wesleyan University Press, Middletown CT and used by permission.

Excerpt from *Trauma And Recovery* by Judith L Herman, MD, copyright © 1992. Reprinted by permission of Basic Books, an imprint of Hachette Book Group, Inc.

ISBN: 978-1-6255-7175-5

Published 2025 by Black Lawrence Press.

Printed in the United States.

for my family

& for my mother

Contents

The conflict between the will to deny horrible events and the will to proclaim them aloud is the central dialectic of psychological trauma.

—Judith Herman, *Trauma and Recovery*

Incunabula as the Light Turns

In the story I keep trying to tell, there's a woman
handcuffed in the driveway.
She's thrashing against the officers, cursing, spitting

on them, her breath rising in the cold air until it
disappears, and they shut the Charger's backseat door.
Six of us kids are watching

from her bedroom window overlooking
the garage, our faces
shocked with police light.

When my brother and I were smaller, we found
a bird in the backyard that had pecked itself
raw, almost featherless, and continued

digging into its own quivering flesh.
We rushed inside to tell our mother,
her hands still dripping with sink water

when she swept us into her arms and said
to stay away from the diseased thing,
there was nothing we could do.

Conch

Bright against the tiki bar's
dark wood, a tiny ocean
sloshes inside. Technically

a summation of all sounds
perpetrated in the bar
scrambles to a wash of echoes

intimating waves—a wide lonely
pressed to one's ear, the finely furred
tunnel twisting into the brain.

Among the stuff the conch hears
and, by hearing, erases:

I bet you still on
Mommy's credit card, the man
says to him. *Sucklin' them fat teats.*

Can't even help yourself
she taste so good...

Compartments. Rooms inside rooms. Inside
his chest thrums
the dumbest song. The song is

tequila. He was feeling on edge.
He was drinking not
because of what the man

makes him remember—

a basement bedroom. He is lying in bed. It's dark except for the black-light in which glows a felt poster of a black panther, yellow eyes, open jaw. Bamboo beads for a door trickle like rain as they split. His mother, wasted, her nightgown halfway down her shoulders, her chest. Her nipple, the shape, the dim color in the doorway, the beads behind. She does not come closer. She says something he can't decipher. He stares at the panther's teeth. She speaks. The world gets trapped inside.

In the bar he smashes the conch across the man's unbearable mouth.

Landscape as Time Machine

Still, there are things we can't reverse.

Moon's counter-clockwise spin. Oyster marsh
pinned down by winter.

I turn them, these things, in my mind

this way. Across the far bridge, a radio tower
disperses its red

in diffuse, silent blinks. A signal. A burning

withdraws. Repeats. And whatever glides
beneath the blip, its canvas of bog water

congealing reeds, whatever burrows

in the mud chill, the mud-sunk
medical needles, burrs, cardboard, tin cans,

orphaned hooks, besmeared candy wrappers—

the defiled scrape
of this place.
        Egg Harbor—

my *incunabula*—cocoon, cradle, swaddling

clothes, winding-sheet—no one chooses
the metaphors they need.

When a pain is unspeakable
it speaks until the grave.

Mere Atmosphere

I looked it up: the internet's data centers are sleepless
white rooms filled with hives of hard drives

cooled by towers of ground water. Photographic satellites
stitch together fragments to approximate

the whole, which tonight is
this Google map of the neighborhood I grew up in,

the old house that holds its dark inside
like a fist or a skull.

* * *

On the quasi-3D map,
the backyard pool I often tried, for fun, to drown
my brother in
                        is uncovered, clear, the shape pinched
in the middle, like a cell in mitosis, splitting
apart from itself...
                        I zoom in further, but
can't see through the house's roof, to the kitchen
where my mother
is helping him with homework, banging
her fist on the paper. Eraser shavings

cling to the greasy table. *Sorry, sorry.* He winces
as I divide to smaller selves, shrinking
to the basement…
                    You need a therapist,
a stranger, not unintelligent, once said to me,
meaning, *Why so much*
unsatisfying opaqueness?

Stranger, I'll tell you this:
it was night. After,
there was a hole in the wall
the size of my brother's skull.

* * *

Clicking, clicking, clicking, clicking—
in a data center, a light goes on,
a machine starts breathing.

Often I've seen what is not visible
but pulls like a strange gravity
in my skull. Often I've blamed myself

for the rust inside the perfect steel.
If, looking through air, we can't
see air, still we're breathing

like machines, motion

inverted, repeating—*it happened now*
it's over; it's over now

it's happening—a light goes on
in my fist, gnawing between
my knuckles. I'm trying to
open it.

Family Portrait

The freak blueberry bushes my mother demanded
be replanted from the lawn to the backyard—

my little brother's darting between them, filling
a steel pot, when the sprinklers start to hiss

from their holes, exploding up to spray. But what he hears
are snakes, drops the pot, all the berries spilling

into the bare dirt and sand flooding to mud. No grass,
not yet, this is a week before my father rolls out sod,

the heap of mulch still steaming like a dead woolly
mammoth in the driveway, smell of rot and all

the animals lacing through it—field mice, silver-specked
lizards burrowing into the mound...

My brother cries all afternoon, on and off,
through Chinese take-out, brushing teeth, now

night like a blindfold with large eyeholes
pulled over his head. I'm sneaking a peppermint

from the pantry for him when I catch my father
driving his foot through the kitchen wall,

our mother still not home from her dayshift working tables at the casinos, *working for dirt,* she says.

My Mother's Computer

In the sheer sloth of another school night, another
social studies assignment, the first time
I was allowed to use it—the same one

she adopted my siblings from, auctioned off
her dolls but, more often, bought more to put
customized outfits on—the bulky black Dell

perplexed me, like looking into a pond and seeing
vague movements underwater. *Whisper*
a name—
                                George, I entered, pecking
the keys, sheepish, like my mother would, with only
index fingers. Then *Bush,* for the project I would

complete like the example child I had deemed
myself. Images of a confused-looking man
filled the screen, useful to me, though I already knew

before I knew to stop myself what I was
about to do—glancing left, then right. My mother
upstairs somewhere. The house

uncannily quiet. The communal
privacy of her computer room—interrupted
only by a dusty moth assaulting the overhead light.

His running-mate, *Dick*, I typed, clicked
Search—no *Cheney*, no pause—unwinding
a jack-in-the-box, her computer screen bursting

with anatomical diagrams and plush
abdominal down—bronze men trapped
in the gallery's rigid grid, little rooms

in which, stiff, they held themselves like trophies
as I was holding myself, astonished
in the glow of that rectangular world.

Self-Portrait as Boyhood Erection

& this is how you wear a sock
over your head: stretch
      & cotton-sweat, lips
coy as petals,
         whetted then struck
           by a barbarous tugging—
smell of grass,
         of cinnamon,
    of aftershave still on scuttling
hand. I live in denim musk,
    a clam unshelled &
         flowering
in classroom, locker room, bathroom stall—
I live to enthrall & be enthralled.
I live like most things: a burgeoning,
           then pink-shrink & loll.

Scull Bay

Under the moon wrapped in gauze,
with one white bird out in the marsh hay
stalking shimmers beneath the water,
my little brother and I are filling beach buckets
with junk from the salt mud: silt-clogged
pocket lighter, stopwatch
stopped, an otherwise pretty doll
head, eyelids bobbing seizure-like
when I tilt it in my hand. Our plan
is to sell the stuff roadside, buy
escape tickets with the money, we think—
we oldest two who can hardly
stand each other, me often pinning his arms
under my knees, jabbing his chest, calling
the dog to lick his open mouth
while our mother shouts from the computer
upstairs, or argues with our father
about a broken door hinge, the unwanted family
reunion next month, his garage-hidden
handle of vodka. Cigarette smoke
chokes her closed office like the fog swirling
blue over the bay-tide here
drawn into itself like a secret.
Half an hour into walking, my foot finds
in the mud the point-tip
of a gnawed-up jig, its decapitated hook
piercing my flip-flop an inch

into my left heel,
flesh ripping inward and oozing. But I can't
pull it out. Limping, useless, I call
the search off, less than half a bucketful each,
upsetting my brother who still
wants to keep looking, not knowing
for what exactly, in the trash and sand
running longer than we can follow, through the marsh
with its lone white bird who won't
turn her head, the shelved moon too wounded
to blink, distant, precious
as my brother's life is to me, our lives
to each other, though we can't
see it, not yet.

Woods Again

Already late, miles away, we find an abandoned couch
camouflaged by dead leaves, and my little brother

belly-flops onto it, lies there babbling at me
as the leaves shiver in the wind running

and tree trunks dim to silhouettes seeming taller
now, faceless with bark. A woodpecker

invisible somewhere in the branches
drumming like regret. My brother's saying *Not yet,*

but I'm saying we've got to go or the light
will strand us, saying *It's getting colder. I'll make you*

a snack. I'm saying *C'mon, stupid,*
gutterslut, scrub, c'mon, saying so many things I forget

what I've already said and say them again. *Just*
a little longer, he says, burying his face

in the cushion's cracked gray above the ground rattling
leaf shreds, the dirt darkening

blacker black. *I can't go back there,*
he might've said—but by then I'd already left.

Incunabula Descending the Stairs

Somewhere between the first move and
the last, my mother orders a chandelier online

but doesn't know how to install it.
It's sometime late November: early dark,

the day going out, barbeque in the oven
starting to fill the house with an odor my brothers

wrestling in the basement will soon smell,
bringing them pounding up the stairs.

On a ladder in the foyer, she's replacing just the crystals
from the old, wrought-iron chandelier,

stringing each new, tear-shaped gem
into the curve of a black hook,

so its empty weight dangles there for dusk
to scatter through it, slanting from the windows

into flecks of bleached rainbow sent
slowing across the walls like a song fading

into the memory of a song.
Perched on a high rung, she looks a moment

at me descending the stairs, my gangling body
wrapped in a blanket, hair like a mop,

and for a brief time, our gazes cross
at the same height, eye level and speechless, looking

into someone else's life that is also our own life.
I don't know what keeps her mind stiff

but spinning like a weather vane in a storm.
It's unclear if she feels—quiet as she is, watching those jewels

suspend—the strange intrigue
of seeing through them her own body as it might look

afterwards: a shadow, distorted,
spilling its shape across the floor.

Crabwise

The derelict box trap in the brackish creek
        behind his grandparents' campground RV,
padded with slime-reeds and a thick dark
    stinking mud, was fun to

    poke with a stick
from the footbridge above. Having been kicked
        from home for the weekend, *and don't
come back,* why—

he could hardly recall now that the trap's cull ring
        had released a chewed up
croaker into free-float
    procession on the water's leafed surface. So he kept

    prodding, teased out a small green crab,
half-rotted, nipped at
        by whatever else in there
had been living until it starved too, bait

for the next, kept going like that, more food
        for the crab hatchlings
swarming the cage somehow this early
    in spring, a milk-plume of teeth, feasting, tiny

    enough he'd mistaken them
for water bugs until just then, and thought: brushed chitin

where the pincers will be.
He put down his stick.

Little aliens, lovesick—
       cast off, stricken
with growing—their charged
   larval bodies molting.

Incunabula over Knobby Scars

Hold out your hands, my mother says
in the dim-lit box of our bathroom,

windowless, the wallpaper a thicket
of coiled vines, roses

flattened in bloom, buds
stunted. It's night. The tile's cold

as chemical burn. She wants to guide
her stainless-steel tweezers

to my knuckle, to the lip
of another wart. We've done this

before: I've bitten the chapped inside
of my cheek as she yanked, scraped

without rage, her grip
calm on the flaw, exacting

the fix, while the sink's basin
dribbled with color. But the roots

only deepened, sprouted back,
burrowed down closer to the vein

to defy her, I want to say, though she
was beyond ordinary resistance

or pain—in the bathroom lamplight
her shadow covers my waiting face.

Hold out your hands, she says.

The Dogshark

Goblin fish zagging the line
a third time, illegal to keep—
we'd thrown her back twice already,

though the catch-cooler was still empty
and we were overheating in an ash-cover
of smog, the day dropping from us swell by

swell. Easy to blame her for my uncle's
cursing, heaving the rod back too hard
and tripping into his own drift-net feathered

with lures. It hooked his thigh—
a centipede of blood crawled down his leg
through the ginger mess of hair

as he pulled her in, gripping the neck
to avoid the venom-barbed fins, threw
her down and poured the rest of his beer

over her eyes' slimed gold. I didn't focus
on his violence, but her gills flaring open,
slits thin as a fingernail's edge, deep enough

I could've touched her guts through them.
And by the time I realized my uncle
was returning from the cabin below

with a baseball bat, banging it along the floor,
the boat tipping side to side,
and I started screaming *Throw her back, throw*

her back—he had already made up his mind.

* * *

In nightmares, I'm on that boat again,
but it's *my* hand, *my* row of knuckles
clutching the bat, knocking the head

into loose-scattered scraps of squid-bait,
my thigh still bleeding as I limp
nearer to the dogshark—and *she's*

me too, holes where my lungs should be,
clotting glue-like, purple from the inside out.
I can't breathe. The thought of having a child

terrifies me. Terrifying that someone like me
could watch himself bringing the bat down
and speak too late,

watch himself become something else.

Chapter

Haze like a bad dream brought down: highbeams
straight through the velvet dark. But not very
far—downhill, the son's shortsighted; and uphill only
sky: overcast, starless. Maybe a mile before he's
home—a night out watching some horror flick
he didn't want to see, and anyway won't entirely
remember, no DVD re-watched in six months, no
token or marker for this evening out of hundreds
insisting—*this, don't forget this*—though not a single
detail precise enough to place: no color of the door
slammed shut and like a cut reopened, the knob
breaking; no phrase yelled back across a room, just
yelling, the sound of it. Who hit first? Which pair
of shoes did the mother in her nightgown or jeans
throw at him when he came back again, shaking, armed
with nothing, the windows so fogged from outside
that even their furious bodies dissolved, unrecognizable.

Egg Harbor

Back before the season of pills and grill smoke,
before my youngest brother's head

gets beat through drywall and into a stud.
Before the framework of that house is even up,

half-built lumber ribcage, the beams dampened
red in morning fog and one bending

slightly when my mother pushes into it hard
with her whole body, saying *It's got to be*

tested. Before the digging, the foundation
carved into the plot cleared of all the larger

trees—great oak, white cedar—toppled
and rolled by the jaw of a dozer. Before the comb

of saws splitting the harvested trunks,
the harvester and his truck, his cigarette long lit.

I can go hours like this,
putting plants back in the ground.

Listen, Love

I never asked for yard work or its sadnesses,
August days filling green plastic barrels to the brim

with weed stalks, roots, unlucky worms. Evenings,
I coiled bare fingers around the furred blades stubborn

to survive. I had my stubbornness, too. My skin thinly
peeling, hours and hours I filled the barrels anyway, dragged them

wheel-less and scraping on the sidewalk, because my father told me to,
half a mile through powerlines scrub to the dump site.

My mother slept all day or shopped endlessly online for dolls.
At night, the foyer's tall curio glowed, glass shelves

populated with the miniature faces. She'd sit on the floor, staring
up at them. Her fingers pinched at the Berber carpet's tight threads.

Each day returned to me unharmed. Each day
some morning thing came, beating its wings. My father, who stayed

long on the riding mower for peace—I still hear him calling me
away from that house, to the backyard or needy lawn, his voice

straining, half-muffled by sliding door glass.
Even now, everything in me lifts to follow it.

Pastoral

The bay-tide at dusk is a tired muscle.
My little brother and I sword-fight

wiffleball bats in the front yard. On the porch,
our uncles drink and smoke and don't

speak. They've been watching the marsh—
tar-black mud, skeletal reeds stuck

in the dropping bank slope. Our father
is up there too, watching, chalked eyes

like an egret's, lids pinned open as with sleep-
deprivation, the strained pupils hollowing

deeper. He's waiting for any small shift
in the saltgrass: wind-drag, a splash, turtle's head

breaking for air.

Incunabula After Last Bell

Pressed to an unseen edge, I held my thumb out
to the wheels of strange men, and let them
drive me from high school home,

though I knew the wooded roads well enough to walk
if I chose. In this scene, I'm soaked
from rain. My soccer cleats squish like barbed sponges

as I climb into the beater truck of a poorly shaven
construction worker, artificial dandruff
shedding black from the ceiling foam

into my hair. What was I after, getting in?
Streetlights doused in the side mirror,
the shrinking, electronic burn

of a gas station sign, rickety trees, the damp
rasping leaves—for all my looking back, he turns
the wrong direction, and keeps driving.

* * *

In another version, it's my mother driving me
the wrong direction home. The rain
evaporates. Darkness gathers

in the passing branches of oak.

The road is pocked with flattened frogs
I try to look away from.
Geese, unembarrassed,
are still honking at the retention pond,

late September, just before
their complete departure, the water green
with last scats, my mother humming
her heartbroken ballads from the driver's seat.

The falling sun divides her face.
The leaves are already weak, each
scrabbling against the inevitable
magnetic blaze of genes.

Still

Hard to recall my little brother's failed attempt
without the moon's white ash

through pinholes in the wind-tossed
tissue of pitch pine needles, porous,

alien as a netting of gills overhead.
I've followed our night path back to the abandoned

living room set, where he's already swallowed
the bottle of ibuprofen, extinguished

his flashlight, capsized belly-down, groaning
incoherent as mist

on the wet couch cushions. He doesn't
recognize me. Doesn't jerk his leg when I grip

above his knee and clamp. I'm shouting his name
in circles. I'm shouting his name years later

still a child shaking my brother alive
in these woods, needing his sneaker-prints

in the damp ground, needing the padding of needles
cut loose, haphazard between scale-bark trunks

and ghosts hidden from sight—squirrel skull,
dead syringe—needing a way out

a way deeper through.

Vision at the Blue Hole in Winslow Woods

The pines drop a cone or two into the pool.
They're throwing buoys
to the woman I see facedown in the freezing
bottomless water.
The night's fog-tangle thickens with iron, listening.

No bat chatter or deer rustle. No fish skitter.
No insects swirling infinitesimal
shadows overhead. If she
is dead, if she is dying—does it matter which?
My feet curl like claws in the sugar sand. I think
she is my mother. But I can't see her face.

My heart's a headcase.
Ghost of her fist pressed
to my sternum she's saying
what she says.
All I can do is listen
as the water's magnetic ruptured surface
clears, if it does. The pine cones
bloat like ulcers, then sink,
sucking me down with the voice of my mother.

Anniversary

Tonight a storm scrambles the clocks
and I'm sixteen again on the bank of the Tuckahoe,
throwing rocks into the starless water

while Doug, still alive, rummages the construction site
for things to set on fire—soiled rag, concert flyer,
bird's nest flung in the scrub-reeds. Soon he's

found something new under the bucket loader,
but his yelling blends with the tire sounds
funneled down like shell-echoes

from the highway overpass behind us. I sink
another rock as he comes closer, corpse
of a bird dangling from his unsmashed hand,

a highbeam's yellow wash across his face a moment
before it flees the unburned
skin. He says *Hold it for me*

pulling the lighter out of his right jean pocket
with the thumb and knuckle that bend
when he spins the striker, and the wing of the bird

I can't save, already dead, can't
douse in black river water, catches—
and we watch the flame climb the feather-tips

into the hollow quills, where the air,
trapped, has nowhere left to go.

Matthew Shepard

Connor King's dad walked in too quick
without knocking, caught him
in the act, witnessed the slow-mo

clip of cosplay lesbian duo
everyone at school seemed to hear about
overnight. Lunchroom chatter. No kudos—

everyone watched porn, though now he could change
clothes in the locker room's bathroom stall
without the guys talking shit.

Yes, the story, but because it was believed,
I knew the choice I was making
when I unlocked my bedroom door,

and turning the volume higher
for my father passing to hear,
began to arrange the screen.

Bloodworms

Walking shoeless down the inlet's jagging shore, twenty feet out
I saw them

breeding, cellophaned in moon, opening
to larvae shreds, then going limp, shoal water

slick with dimly shimmering husks, reproductive confetti
that wallowed up, smacked of semen on my tongue

like a hot syrup in the dark, familiar, alien. It stunned me; I stumbled
from form into fear of

being small, bursting, like them, to nothing but teeth, skimmering
sudden hunger. I was seeing my

mother, bailed out and broke, checking into the motel room my father had
arranged the week before the custody hearing, and then it came

in cooling, shallow waves, what she
must've thought to herself, confirming her name, taking the key.

Incunabula and the Sound of Cicadas

How many times, really, did my mother's voice
harshen from the darkened concrete stoop?
At the junction of *maybe* and *felt fact,* it seems
not very often, not often at all, though again

I'm headed away, into the rain-sopped woods,
a shaky flashlight in my hand, as mist
confuses the beam and dusk smolders
like a wet smudge of graphite. The corrugated tarp

of pine needles slung above, heavy, drips
warm pollution down my spine. My breath
grinds to a pant. I'm far enough in,
or after, I shouldn't hear her.

But I do. At the bank of the sandy creek
in the deep grammar of water—
she's humming, peacefully, as though
to herself, assembling the bones

of a disjointed life. I know
that clatter. The chinking
together of flints. The tired fire
that carries my body

the same burning that threatens it.
I kick a rock.

I throw a dead beer bottle at a tree trunk,
and the air inside bursts

a bright shrapnel of flying green shards,

a face glinting,
fractured, in each spinning piece.

Elegy After a High School Car Crash

for Doug

Gunshots,
you were saying, fired on the floor above the casino restaurant

your parents worked in, though they hadn't yet met.
Lockdown. Huddled behind the dishwasher's steel

conveyer line, knees touching hers, your father
said—not in his graveled smoker's wheeze,

but his then-voice, still half-belonging to a boy
resembling you—*Think they'll let us snack on the bacon?*

or possibly *My dog is gonna whizz himself
when he hears about this.*

Which sentence was it? that started your life before your life
began, a dream not remembered but, waking, hazy, reaching to twist the
  blinds open, felt.

* * *

We begin in language—
place you've returned to since, still a *person,*
but taking with you the wrecked car, empty bottle

in some nameless dumpster. And took my functioning
though I'm alive, complaining *snooze* on the alarm, going to school,
  catching bits of
news from the ongoing world. Last week, a truck in Philly barreled
  through the side

of a daycare building, killing two kids, a teacher. Everyone in the CarMax
  waiting room
put down their phones to stare at the lone, wall-mounted TV—the air
  so suddenly speechless
audible was this young woman's baby, not really whimpering, but startled

by the new silence, squirming in it
as the woman rocked him—she couldn't have been much older than
  me—saying, saying again, *hush*.

* * *

Walking Margate Beach at night, aimless, vague
rage simmering in our throats, fixed as if

inherited almost, though shared, *understood*. The air
warm-wet, stars a radio silence we were

wading through, ocean murmur
restless to one side. The story of your parents meeting,

the scene—not remembered, but imagined—

occurred to you, it seemed, the way a lighter's scraped heat

quivers beneath a cigarette, igniting, releasing
what is dormant there: upstairs in a casino twenty years ago, a bullet

ricocheted off a slot machine
clanging sounds, and sent the lucky symbols reeling.

The Bat

In that slow and sinking hour, night
driving, it was you, dear loner, dear
nocturnal almost-bird, but not,
black chevron unpinned and slivering
the air as though gravity were more
a hinge to swoop than a load to fly—
it was you surprise nosediving,
ricocheting off my windshield
and down into the shoulder weeds
behind, leaving before me a bloodless scuff—
smearing worse with cleaner fluid
before the wipers could rise across, as I took
the next curve too hard, almost
flipped, couldn't even yell the name
of the knot muting me
in blitzed aloneness
that you also must've known, blinked
into, forgetting cave, motel
rafter, tree limb, car,
all in this apart.

Home

Summer's end, in this exhalation of reeds
and mire scent, you can skirt
away from nothing, with no one to
lie to, or persuade though meaning well,

alone at the RV campground lake,
slouched in a folding chair, dipping
your hand into the cleaned-out
spackle bucket filled with bait minnows

sloshing in a knot of silver,
a knot attempting to untie itself,
the reeling thin metallic bodies,
daylight left still flecking off scales.

You'll sit there for hours, quiet
through a slow burn sinking
beneath the pines, lake water
blackening to a version less itself,

the surface a burnish of other things
ignited—distant trailer lamp, fleeing
golf cart's taillight, and brightly
distorted: liquid-tinsel moon

flattened, trapped all night in a slow
drift across the water,

as though ensnared in a net
and struggling loose like

your life, there is no
other way, you must try to salvage it.

Male Pattern

Early fade, it has come to this, in the spring
of my twenty-second year, scrounging
in the insufficient sink light,
scrounging through the fresh, unwanted space
for an explanation
                      from the fallen strands,
the mutinous
loosening, then gone. Outside, the huge
magnolias have bloomed late
and white beneath starlight, the dark
green leathery leaves thick
                      as pauldrons, hexing
silver pebbles from their polish
and flinging them at the window, soundless,
so, turning from the mirror, from my own
reversed face:
                      the hallucination of moths,
electric and mute, in the night
still darkening.

* * *

Down, in the under-threading
of nucleotides, twisting
down from my mother's father,

in his pattern that is also
my pattern, there
                    he is, still
living, no hair, a box of cigars
tucked under his arm as he slips

out the garage, into the oil-
black air not yet
ruptured by police sirens, officers

knocking, pushing
open the unlocked door—
his wife in the kitchen only

just before, releasing
the telephone cord
from around my mother's neck.

* * *

Call once and hang up, then call again—he told
his mistresses. But my mother kept
receipts from his work pants
stored in a shoebox beneath her bed...

When she unfolded them crinkling
apart like the wings of dead insects
for her mother to see, proof—

the disbelieving room

turned on its side, furious, then blue
light in the window glass—

does violence live in the genes,

their story telling itself
in the dormant voice
of a seed,

muffled behind husk, there, between
my ears,

my ears
ringing and ringing.

* * *

The years between
constrict. At dinner, my mother, testifying.
She's the casual refugee, history-

keeper runaway
now laundry-queen, changing
loads between coating batches of raw chicken

with *Shake 'N Bake,* sipping

always on a glass of wine, swirling the ice.
At night, her erratic machines

sputter on fabric softener
satiny as moon, toxic soups of bleach, detergent,
routine, TV. She sets the glass

down again,
the hot iron fuming, her face lit
blue with crime movies, actors

she recognizes from other shows, other roles, faces
distorted by a cathode,
shifting, familiar as her own.

* * *

To my left, in the half-image of the bathroom window,
my hair now white
dandelion fluff,

each feathery strand
floats the trace, bulbous face
of a family member—some I didn't

know I remembered, and all of them
yelling in the unintelligible language
of anger—snarling, nipping

with smokers' teeth, threatening
to sink the first
crumbling bite.

And beyond that reflected me,
the dark yard
of anxiety I seem to stand in—all of it

erupts in gust:
the magnolia, grass, loose dirt
weighing the grass down to root, the little

dumb moths
the color of wishfulness, tumbling—
and one by one—mother, grandfather—then

in clumps, the seed stalks
of my family,
my hair, whips off, spiraling

the screams diminishing away
from my newly shining scalp.

Incunabula Just Before

The courthouse garden, during the last
rounds of my mother's trial, pleasant
side yard to justice, was throbbing

with pollen, each split-open flower
a slow-motion sneeze
as my brother wiped his hand,

snotty, across the bench's arm, licked
what remained, and slicked the spit
on his too-large dress pants. I didn't

know the names—black-eyed Susan,
maybe hyacinth—but I knew the colors
obscured a pattern underneath

only insects could see, their eyes
compounding frequencies
I couldn't fathom, as the midday sun

struck the garden a near shadowless
glow, and bees droned from petal
to petal. I sat on the bench,

trying to guess the designs hidden
from me, until it was half
past, and I was summoned

back to the courtroom, my turn,
to testify against her.

Palimpsest

Afterwards, until the boy was done, the woman guarded
the bathroom door, and though it was closed almost enough

that she couldn't see in, or him out, it still emitted
a vertical strip of light she sometimes held

her ear to. And later, down the street, summer dusk, someone
must've been talking, or at least the boy

heard someone talking, disembodied, in the low
skitter of last year's leaves, saying *No*

roses ever grew. But who? and what did they mean?
Not here, he agreed—where ducks

gangled in small flocks
stupid and rainbow-sheened on the retention pond

while he watched, counting them, trying not to think
of the house, the open kitchen, the empty box

of chocolate laxatives on the Formica island, and the little product-
picture on front that she

had shown him, pointing at the glossy image—almost the same color
as the floating layer of pond sludge

splitting inward like a membrane as beaks pierced down
and the tree line above—tousled, darkening—

eased shadows across the water.
No roses ever grew from her perfume bottle,

though it carried the scent—the woman
soaked a cotton ball, scrubbed the boy's exposed,

bloated stomach—the rubbery, soft skin
and the hardly-visible hairs that covered it. She complained

of the smell coming from
inside him, though *he* couldn't smell it himself, hiding behind

the water heater in the unfinished
basement room, skipping meals, sticking a finger

down his own throat. When she told him to measure
the chocolates out again—*five, six*—

he pushed, one at a time, into his mouth
those waxy squares that could pass for candy.

Ars Poetica

The scene comes as a heat shimmer does:
a young summer, sitting with my father
on my grandparents' drooping porch, watching

an egret down by the marsh's unmarked edge—
jilted bride with a backwards
neck-crook, stilted white as if for the sake

of brightness. She's searching between
cattail stalks for small movements to
jab at, plodding over the soft mud, then peering

so long at the same raised shadow, her body
poised, otherworldly almost, her beak
a needle-point blade, that my father

has named her Patience. And when
my mother calls from the house, disgruntled
at something my grandmother said—in the memory,

always just then, as my mother's voice
rings out in the hot swamp air,
Patience snaps down, spears a frog, and swallows.

Incunabula Standing Above Myself

Yet it's my own face that ruptures
when I toss in the rock.

Rare sun, drifts of pewter riffling,
sound of people talking, trailing off...

Image, apparition. Not a bridge
but like a bright chill of water shifting.

Yes, I saw her do that
to him, the child is answering

the lawyer. *Yes, I saw blood.*
I didn't do anything.

Night Fragments from Underbrush

Soggy running shoe. Snapple cap with its "real
fact" on the underside, defaced
unreadable, lost. Glittery lip gloss like bottled-up dream. Mood ring
immutable. Dissevered hook from a bungee cord still
tangled around a branch.
                              Little Brother, I've wound myself
hours at a time through these woods, scavenging with
a bucket, thoughts clattering
metal scraps at the back of my skull.
The waking dream repeating: I hold

my open hand where she's about to drive your
head into the kitchen wall;
but with my palm as cushion, there's no hole, no blood,
no dent in the hidden, wooden beam,
no mother screaming at her own shaking hands,

as if by dreaming you might be spared—
no, there's no one left here to save.
I will bury this ache in the dirt with the rest,
for someone else to find.

Incunabula, Mother Tongue

My mother—blogger, doll addict
cyber queen, sniper
at the eBay auction computer screen—

mixed her idioms.
From the get-go, for example,
became *From the gecko*

when she said it. *Not the sharpest*
bowling ball in the shed.
He side-blinded me. Shithead thinks he's cool

as mustard. Thinks he's right up my sleeve.
I escaped from New Jersey
for college, which *opened up a whole nother*

can of germs. In emails I wrote: *Professor,*
I'll have to mow it over a little longer.
Professor, without a question of a doubt.

I didn't realize I made switches too
until I re-read them—a nervous,
first-gen scholarship student—

as I'm sure my mother didn't think
she'd altered anything
in her life. But that's a different chiasmus

for a different line of thought,
not for nights like this one, alone
and happy mostly, my heart *at the peck and call,*

though, of those suburban woods
of my childhood again—
the ultraviolet yellow feathers

of witch-hazel thicket, serrated
huckleberry leaves—the understory
so dense, tangled to itself, that walking

a straight line becomes
a tight circle, and my mother's voice is mine.

April Begins in My Father's Ear

I leave a message after the tone.
Await the text back: *Sorry. Busy. Call soon.*
—your hurried guilt rushing
sideways through each day's fiberglass barbs—my sister, sick
& sleeping beside the Target's dark dumpster
last week, I know. Or Little Brother's finger crushed
beneath the garden rock he'd been running with, like all of us
really, toward you, before he tripped—
the rock being, of course, a rock
but also the dense problem of itself
& another problem you can't solve,

barraged-always Dad of seven of us,
still motherless no matter how old we grow,
steady always sturdy Dad not getting younger, this is
my ode for your new hearing aid, badly needed,
just this month embedded
in your cochlea: cute, Bluetooth stone
that *brrrings* my ringtone
across the myelinated branches
in your head. *Sorry! Hey!*
And I tell you about the oak & dogwood
bursting here in vellus-covered spring,
the small heft of buds swaying
as I walk to the grocery. *You're
just calling because you're bored,* I hear you say
before you say it, though you answered, though I have your ear, I am in

your ear, we have a tone, it is spring, & you can hear me.

Cheesecake Factory

I can't get over the fact of your clean smile,
your bowl of jambalaya pasta,
even as a germ of pain beds down
in my lungs. I was folding jeans as a "model"
in the strip mall's manufactured musk.
& afterwards, in the lush vacancy
of the nighttime lot, floodlit after warm rain,

beneath its dome of electricity & sheen—
I held the hand of the first boy I liked,
our digits interlocked in percolating fire

when a shock unzipped across
my shoulder, the axis
of my neck, & we turned to face
a xenon blast of headlights,
a black pickup
following us.
                    Mist
across its windshield. Light jagged across
that mist. We walked. The engine growled closer
then farther as we cut through a corridor of SUVs
until the pickup approached again
around the bend, & my shadow, as if sudden
in the bright blur, grew taller than I was.

Can I say? I love very much being
at this table at the Cheesecake Factory with you,
& can I tell you about the rainy night,
the engine sound &
the human eyes I imagined behind
the truck's glass, its blitz of light

behind me everywhere I go.

I say, *Don't let go of my hand.*

Babysitting My Adolescent Brother

When again he's powdered the couch with flour
or smeared the bathroom mirror

with the turd he scooped back out—
his brackish grin watching me

go in, after—
when I've scolded him and pointed

up to his room, escorted him there,
clicked the door shut. I think again

of Emerson's brother, Bulkeley, in McLean Asylum,
taken out then put back in, who took the train

to Mont Vernon—impromptu toodle-oo—
collecting names, door by door,

for the singing class he'd teach
until he was returned, like a mislabeled package, home

before anyone could learn
a thing. My own brother, the one now sitting

on his bed behind the door I closed,
was driven home like that

on mornings he, ten years old, naked as dirt, rose
before the birds began

shuffling in the yard's imposing oak,
and crossed the main road that wore

blemishes of flattened squirrels,
went porch to porch, slurping the lukewarm dregs

from beer cans forgotten overnight.
He knocked on doors to express his thanks.

What a nice boy, they'd say, eyebrows raised,
returning him to my father, still groggy

in his boxers, as my brother, exposed,
flashed from the foyer to the stairs

back to his room where he's crying
on his bed, and this bafflement keeps

walking me back, to open the door again.

Incunabula, Fever

Maybe it was just the bright snow's incandescence
    that burned through my sheer drapes
and woke me up, and kept burning spectral across the room

    as I opened my phone's inbox to a text message
from my mother, unrecognized
    number borrowed from another boyfriend, time-stamped

some slurred hour too early to call. It had slipped in
    unannounced while I slept, bearing a picture of a younger me
I almost didn't recognize, or almost *could*, grinning

    from a swing set, captioned as if from a happy childhood
—*can you believe this?* I couldn't
    swallow, my throat raw as bark—the phrase

a splinter in my tongue rubbing against my teeth...
    I *believe* in miles and miles of powerlines.
Squirrel spines. Dog droppings. Deer prints

    in loam. The urine tang
of rotten grass clippings piled
    high enough to house a colony of skinks. Metallic

hissing at dusk, flashing silver tails.
    Shadows of moth-flutter shrinking as night
pries open its beak. The harsh links

between transmission towers. The sleeved white fire
of black cables running a distance
    farther than any child could try. This kid,

this kid in my phone in my shaky hand
                                    is quivering
beneath the cold morning's bleach-bone searing light.

Trying to Pray

I close my eyes and think of water.
—James Wright

Okay, I'm thinking of water—
its metallic drip, its ripples
darkening the silver bowl
of the brain, making me nervous, or
is that not what Jim meant?
You know this landscape,
don't you, night-dissolved
kaleidoscope of fog behind fog
and the soundless blare of headlights
burning the layers up
the mountain in alternating curves
of road. It runs until it runs
out. What tense are we in? My brother
is enlisting. My friend's brother
enlisting. Enlisted. Will enlist. *Would be*
fun to shoot people, maybe.
Who taught him this? And him?
And him? But you
must know this forward and
back already, living here, you
live here, don't you? I close
my eyes, try to think of water
but see instead the old photograph's
faded desert, my uncle
shirtless, young
as my brother is now, a rifle's strapped

silhouette, depthless
at his side. His grin, it's ordinary—
it's him in there—
he's looking at us—
as he props his boot
on the stripped and blackened Iraqi.

Night of the Bomb-Faced Boy

Pierced, I shut down my phone,
the screen's careless news,
drove the road's wet echo
beyond myself and only
past the state line north
before slowing, crumpling
to the shoulder, to the sagging fence—
for what—to sit
on the damp hill, feeling
the easy guilt? I did
until the horse's snort,
its stamping sound,
the huge dark eye
I stood to meet, flecks of fallen moon
liquid there, and there
in it, the Me I saw:
small, astonished—seen.
The seeing was not human. There was no
more accurate shame. Pricks
of stars on the muddy ground.
Cheat grass, thistle weed's purple tufts
knee-height swaying in soft wind.
The horse breathing. The horse, as if sensing
my need, drew back in
to nuzzle my hand.
I couldn't bear to let it touch me.

After the Fight

Never mind there is no place that is not this place. Begin

with a landscape: fog hovers over the long bend of marsh.

I know.

Kayaks, a few—bright & docked—but there's one rope

vacant, its knotted end drifting in place in the slow current.

So someone (or two) must be out on the water at this strange hour

of overflow, morning sheen, & muck. Come closer to me.

It's my favorite thing, imagining the comings and goings.

& why. & why not. A destination intimates want.

Put your hand on the back of my neck. The

mooring of your hand is what I want.

One Small Change

I was suddenly ill as the rattling bus
curved around the mountains'
repeating elbows
toward the distant summit's tourist village,
last breath before three hours of ancient stairs
crumbling up to green ruins.
To steady myself,
I muttered the memorized fragments
of old poems. *We look at the world once.*
Taciturn, oblivious. I repeated them
for forty minutes or so, until the spell
expired, and the glass ball of pain
in the bloated cradle of my stomach
shook the poems' grip on my clenched attention
and the passing rusts, grassy wavering of
pastures, cliffside, andenes, running streams
loosened, broke open, refracted
into something unexpected—
the rosary prayer I had finally memorized
in childhood, bead by bead, to protect
my hands from the volunteer mom
CCD teacher who paced stork-like
at the head of the classroom, surveying
the grid of melamine desks the color
of a flock of Manila folders,
my legs already quivering
though I was just becoming awake

to my internal situation. She possessed
the expected vengefulness, slapping
with her neon-pink plastic ruler
the clumsy, unremembering knuckles
of my left hand (because she had seen
such a punishment
on TV?), the pale summits and valleys
of my hand deepening red and white
as the beads I should've known by then
how to pray by.

I had no such beads
on the bus, but the mossy geography
of the words of the prayer
like stepping stones surfaced
from the flooded landscape
of my brain where the murk
and water that covers
everything receded to issue,
after decades, in front of me
a path: Hello,
how art thou! who art in Heaven!, hallow
be thy, thy will be, on Earth, give us, and
then the classroom around the prayer
which had formed the prayer to begin with
formed itself again where the undefined
and twiggy gay boy I had been
tried with crayons to create
the illusion of his favorite color "tie-dye"
in the pages of a mass-produced coloring book

filled with handsome depictions of Jesus,
and soon-to-be tie-dyed doves
and tie-dyed execution crosses,
clenching his legs in a kind of prayer
in the absence of poems,
until, like a tragic sideways benediction
of food poisoning and bad timing
he, I, shit my pants, right there in the church classroom
as the faces of the surrounding kids changed,
as the teacher-mom oversaw
my legs squirming with the question
I would've asked
if not for burying it in my larynx instead
or, rather, burying
only its beginning, *Miss,*
can I go—my hand not shooting up,
knowing what I needed but still not
saying so. Then I remembered
I was on a bus, weaving through mountains
and the vision, if we can call it that,
finally compelled me to turn
to my friend who sat beside me, quite oblivious,
reading Nabokov how I imagine everyone
reads Nabokov by watching clouds
drift in the nearest window instead,
the book open in her lap.

I said, *Please.*
Which plainly meant, *I am dying.*

I was not dying, of course,
merely preferring death,
my body the object again, the soul
in this case
a thin thread in a whirlwind
having no business being where it was
though having no volition either,
so I relinquished
and said thank you for the prayer,
thank you for the classroom, the teacher-
mom and her pacing,
thank you for the poems that were the trouble,
the broken ringlets, the unbroken
surface of the pond of the poems
that bought me the forty minutes or so
through which the light of time
shattered and burst across the bus
forming the classroom of the Parish of
Elizabeth Ann Seton in Absecon,
New Jersey, reforming as the passing
of language to my dear friend
to the fluent couple in the front row
who convinced the driver to pull over
into one of the villages along the tourist road
where a shopkeeper, thank you, permitted
my *Please, please, please, please,*
my flinging open the door at the rear
for my sheepish body, which is living.

Subnivean

There is enough memory to burrow a life into
if I can't explain.
It's this crust of light that keeps me dangerous:
you seeing the snow, not knowing where to dig.

Python with a Dog Inside It

Poor dog. Chained to the pine behind the camper RV
where else could it go but in?
                              White barb. Placental speckle
unwriggling. & the elastic ligament that walks
the skull, unhinged,
over the dog's tufty head, neck, torso, tail.

There could be Heaven in there.

Pleasure in adrenaline, pleasure in uncoiling
the grip. Pulsed bristles, halogen
leaking from the vacant bocce courts...

But the chain yanks back—tangled around the dog
already in the throat's long slink. & because
the dog, wet, fetal, slides

head-first in, the python with no mechanism
for revision
              is tethered to what it did,
& to the pine whose fan of roots
anchors it to ground, the dog to it.

Everything wears its consequence, extending
beyond itself the visible.
This is what we see.

Pattered mud. Metal bowl, tipped over. Film of water
glinting white. Crisscrossing
                          spike-like shadows
darkening toward morning's old man, the machete
he'll bring, not yet.
All night—

the other world
chained to this world

by its stuff: a dog, a chain, a pine, a python.

The Scientists

The boy was certain he heard them
in the air behind the air—
tinkering on the time machine
                            that would save him
from his sad suburb,
from his father's yard work, the shrubs
nagging with thorns, dirt-smell

beneath his fingernails like the perfume
of servitude. *Take me away!* he flared without
irony, in the empty hold of a chicken coop

deserted in the woods, ribbed dumpster lids
for a makeshift roof, a green plastic lawn chair
his laboratory perch. The machine

before him, though he couldn't see it, brewed
noises from the metal edges
                          polished as an egg—
sounds like: *blork! sploosh!*—
in that room only he knew, where he hid
long afternoons,

hearing the scientists flit
at their workbenches—saying *hmm...* saying *aha!*—
each small breakthrough leading to the next

until, at last, a nebulous weave of wind
shimmered through the pine shavings on the floor;
a storm of sparks burst from the air then
fell to rust. It didn't seem finished,

not then, when the machine's hatch creaked
open to a yawn of blue light.
The boy climbed in

and vanished into the rest of his life.

Talking It Out

for Jordan

On the couch, another scrimmage,
but how to think without, first, an image?

The stomach doesn't separate liquids
from solids, you say, though why say it

like a foot stamping down? It's hard for me
to see, leafing through dog-eared pages

of your medical education, its illustrations
an art all their own, parsed, transmuted

inside the opaque egg of your skull—
maybe I shouldn't argue. Though,

the capillary plexus, you relent,
does absorb *some* fluids before

digestion in the small intestine.
O tangled hammock, belly

of stars, this *plexus*
you've given me, just because?

I have my image. The thought is love.

Notes

p. 1   *The Incunabula Papers*—using early internet memes, fax machines, etc.—created and propagated fictional messages or "clues" from a colony of time-traveling scientists that operated in the Pine Barrens ghost town of Ong's Hat, New Jersey in the late 1960s/early 70s. According to the myth, they vanished to another time and dimension using a machine called "the Egg."

p. 27 Line 1 alludes to Theodore Roethke's poem "Dolor." The title, as well as line 14, borrow language from another Roethke poem, "A Field of Light."

p. 33 The Blue Hole is a clear blue body of water located deep in the Pine Barrens of Winslow, NJ, and was a popular swimming spot in the 1930s. A number of legends exist: that it is bottomless with powerful downward currents, the water is freezing cold year-round, and the Jersey Devil is especially active in the area.

p. 70 The poem's title alludes to the image of Omran Daqneesh that gained media attention in the US in 2016.

p. 72 The poem borrows fragments from Louise Glück's "Nostos" (*"We look at the world once."*) as well as Larry Levis' "The Widening Spell of the Leaves" (*"Taciturn, oblivious,"* "broken ringlets," and "unbroken surface of the pond").

Acknowledgments

Thank you to the journals and publications in which the following poems first appeared, sometimes in earlier versions:

The Adroit Journal: "Conch," "Egg Harbor," "Python with a Dog Inside It," "Still"
AGNI: "Mere Atmosphere"
Alaska Quarterly Review: "Landscape as Time Machine"
Anthropoid: "Self-Portrait as Boyhood Erection"
Beloit Poetry Journal: "Babysitting My Adolescent Brother"
Best New Poets 2016: "Incunabula, Mother Tongue"
Best New Poets 2019: "Incunabula Just Before"
Birmingham Poetry Review: "The Bat"
Cold Mountain Review: "Woods Again"
Columbia Poetry Review: "Anniversary"
CutBank: "Crabwise," "Listen, Love," "Male Pattern"
Ecotone: "Incunabula Descending the Stairs"
Frozen Sea: "Incunabula over Knobby Scars," "Incunabula Standing Above Myself"
The Greensboro Review: "The Scientists"
Grist Online: "Family Portrait," "Incunabula, Fever," "Ars Poetica"
Gulf Coast: "Scull Bay," "Vision at the Blue Hole in Winslow Woods"
The Journal: "My Mother's Computer"
T Magazine: "Egg Harbor"
Meridian: "The Dogshark"
Northwest Review: "Night of the Bomb-Faced Boy"
RHINO: "Chapter"
Sepia: "Incunabula After Last Bell," "Home"

Volume Poetry: "Elegy After a High School Car Crash," "Pastoral"
Waccamaw: "Incunabula as the Light Turns"
Washington Square: "Bloodworms"

My heartfelt gratitude to Diane Goettel and Black Lawrence Press for their belief in these poems and for their work on *Python with a Dog Inside It*.

I would like also to express my appreciation to the University of Virginia, Vanderbilt University, The Community of Writers, and the Sewanee Writers' Conference for scholarships and fellowships that made this book possible.

For their suggestions, support, and mentorship, dreamiest thanks to Debra Nystrom, Lisa Russ Spaar, Gregory Orr, Rita Dove, Paul Guest, Kate Daniels, Mark Jarman, Beth Bachmann, Mark Bibbins, Hannah Perrin King, Brianna Flavin, Mary Somerville, Derek Pfister, Sophia Stid, Danez Smith, Alina Grabowski, Tiana Clark, Safiya Sinclair, and Jordan Deaner.

And thank you, always, to my father, whose patience and love taught me how to see.

Python with a Dog Inside It, winner of the St. Lawrence Book Award, is **Max McDonough's** debut poetry collection. His poems have appeared in *AGNI, Ecotone, Northwest Review, Best New Poets, The Adroit Journal, Alaska Quarterly Review, Beloit Poetry Journal*, and *T Magazine*, among others. His prose has been nominated for a James Beard Award, and has appeared in *The New York Times, Food52, On the Seawall*, and *Flipboard's '10 for Today.'* He earned his MFA from Vanderbilt University, and now lives in Philadelphia, Pennsylvania.